Be More Than You Are

Be More Than You Are

A Guide to Confident Living

Don Polston

HARVEST HOUSE PUBLISHERS
Eugene, Oregon 97402

BE MORE THAN YOU ARE

Copyright ©1977 by Harvest House Publishers
Eugene, Oregon 97402
Library of Congress Catalog Card Number 77-75404
ISBN 0-89081-071-0

Printed in the United States of America

CONTENTS

Preface

Earl Nightengale said, "Before you can do something you must be something."

It's the "being" which produces the "doing." To be more than you are takes effort, insight and persistence.

Everyone wants something. No matter what it is, you want something: money, peace, love, service to others, a happy marriage, a job, security, or a better home. Dissatisfaction in any of these areas is part of the necessary urge to get what you want. The great secret to get what you need is courage to be more than you are. You must learn to move up and over instead of down and under.

You don't need to know all the answers to all the problems of the world. You must know your own problem and then you can solve your problem. It's the person who keeps solving his problems day by day who will finally arrive at his destination.

Here's hoping, as you read this book, your world will be greater than it is because you are becoming more than you are. You could change your world today if you really think you should.

Happy changing to you as you become more than you are!

Don Polston
Waterloo, Iowa

1

BUILD A
WORKABLE
SELF-CONFIDENCE

Lord, I am unique . . . but I
hope I'm not ridiculous.
I know You can use me
even when I am ridiculous . . .
but I'd rather be radiant.
It's a comfort to know
You are for me.
And that's all I really need
to know,
to have self-confidence.
Amen.

BUILD A WORKABLE SELF-CONFIDENCE

The greatest battle in your life is building a workable self-confidence.

Have you ever said to yourself, "It won't work for me." "I can't do it." "I'm afraid I will look ridiculous." "What if I make a fool of myself?" "What if I'm not as good as people think I am?" "They will never again ask me to do it."

If you believe you are not capable, creative, or worthwhile, your total life will reflect this attitude through failure, disappointment, and heartache.

These are negative foundation stones on which to build a weak, defeated self-confidence; these are the stones which will become a wall of hindrance to successful, happy living.

Why not rephrase these negative statements and decree the very opposite concepts about yourself and your ability.

Let your mind be convinced that people will enjoy a new voice, a new face, and the new concepts which you have to offer. Convince yourself you are unique! Say, "It will work for me!" "I can do it!" "I am not afraid!" "I will look great!" "They will ask me to do it again."

The Apostle Paul understood this when he wrote, "I can do all things through Christ which strengtheneth me" (Philippians 4:13). And the great promise, "If God be for us, who can be against us?" (Romans 8:31). Repeat these over and over in your mind until you believe them yourself.

One little boy said, "If God be for you, everybody else may as well be."

Read the Bible with an open and honest mind. Its promises will give you peace on which to build a workable and balanced self-confidence. What do I mean by a "workable" self-confidence? A workable self-confidence is one that is natural, mature, balanced, whole, and livable. You can live with a workable self-confidence. It makes you feel whole and complete, you have a feeling of worth, yet not of pride.

There is a self-confidence which can be out-of-balance, defeating and disturbing. It can cause negative reactions within you as well as within others.

But workable self-confidence sparks new ideas and energies, causing you to be creative. It will help you to think big. Nothing really big happens to little-minded people who have a defeated self-confidence. When you have a workable self-confidence, you will discover that new charges of energy and vitality will pour into you and through you. You will start to build a new world right where you live. You will discover greater degrees of happiness and usefulness.

Happy hearts are found in busy, self-confident people. You can build a workable self-confidence within you that will bring happiness to your world and the world of others.

2

BE THE PERSON

YOU WANT TO BE

What distorts my fears
to monsters
and my hopes
to wishes?
Lord, what is holding me down?
Show me
and remove the old
scars . . . the old
skeletons.
Clean me up...clean me out.
Amen.

Do you have feelings of depression? Are there times when you consider yourself an under-achiever? Are you bothered by people who have less talent than you and yet appear to be more successful? Perhaps you have a suspicion there may be a better way to live, a more exciting way to achieve than the way you are presently living and achieving.

At a recent motivational breakfast we discussed these questions: What creates desire? What is greed? What is the key that will unlock the doors of success and achievement? One man, a highly successful car dealer said, "It took me fifteen hours a day to accomplish what I can now do in two hours. I am able to accomplish more today because Christ has cleansed from my mind the defeated, distorted fears that crippled me and has forgiven me of my sins."

Others in the group pointed out that desire is the foundation of all effort that produces great results. Desire is the one ingredient which must be in the mind of the individual if he is to become the person he wants to be. Jesus said the same thing when He said, " . . . whatever things ye desire . . ." (Mark 11:24).

What would you say is holding you back from becoming the person you want to be?

Are there old, negative skeletons in the closet of your mind? Perhaps there are old reruns of past failures, fears, or sour images which need to be exposed to the light. Once these old reruns are exposed to the light, the images become blurred and begin to fade. The "film" is no longer good. Most of us not only need converting, we need to have the failure-tendency cleansed from our minds.

This is what Charles Wesley meant when he wrote in one of his hymns, "Take away our bent to sinning." If you will expose your defeated "film" to the light of Christ's love He will destroy the defeated images and they will no longer be able to defeat your efforts.

The failure-tendency, or the "bent to sinning," can be corrected. As this tendency to failure begins to fade, you will discover new hope rising in your heart. Christ is giving you the ability to overcome. You are on your way to becoming the person you want to be!

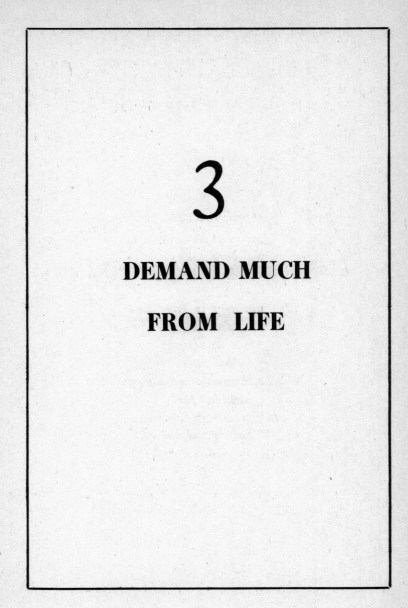

3

DEMAND MUCH
FROM LIFE

Lord, You said,
"Ask what you will...
So, here goes...
But...should I really?
YES!
In Your way, in Your time
do it all.
But, do it little
by little
so I can enjoy the journey
and not feel
stuffed with my desires.
That's good, too.
Amen.

DEMAND MUCH FROM LIFE

How much are you demanding from life? What worthwhile goals are you pursuing? What kind of price are you willing to pay in order to achieve these goals?

Jesus said, " . . . ask what ye will . . ." (John 15:7). "But," you protest, "that seems unreal. That statement simply is not practical!"

The promises of Christ are so big that often they seem too good to be true. The Greek word, "ask," means "Keep right on asking over and over again until you get what you want." How much can you ask for? What are you demanding from life? The greatest mistake you can make is to put a limit on the resources of God in your universe.

It seems everyone believes in unlimited supplies except the church. The world talks of plenty; the church talks of poverty. Industry builds for greatness and for generations to come while the church builds with restraint and only for tomorrow. Is there a limit to the great resources God has planned for you?

Here is an affirmation I read recently: ''And every morning I will say, there's something happy on the way. And God sends love to me. God is the light of my life, the source of my knowledge and inspiration. God in the midst of me knows. He provides me with food for my thoughts, ideas for excellent service, clear perception, and divine intelligence.''

There is not only a spark of divinity in you but also the very nature of God. The Scriptures say, ''...that...ye might be partakers of the divine nature...'' (II Peter 1: 4). This is the hope of the Bible. God's unlimited nature is being joined to yours!

What are you doing to liberate this resource so that it can grow into a great and mighty force in your life? Are you effectively using every opportunity to allow His nature to grow, expand and become the all-consuming force of your life? God's nature is demanding! It demands creativity, growth, expression, and fulfillment.

When you demand much in life you will be surprised how the nature of God will expand to fulfill every need. There is a pressing supply for every pressing demand. Demand much in life!

4

BREAK FREE
FROM THE
TIGER CAGE

What is this cage I have built
around my hopes?
It's a cage of limitation...
limiting productivity
limiting ability.
Why?
Today, I take this self-made
cage apart!
...little by little
I will free
my mind from all prisons.
Amen.

BREAK FREE FROM THE TIGER CAGE

What is a tiger cage? A veteran of the Vietnam war explained to the packed auditorium exactly what it was like to have been locked up in one for four years.

The Communist guerillas operating in South Vietnam had to be constantly on the move through the jungles, fighting each day and capturing prisoners in their conflicts. A big problem was what to do with the prisoners as they moved about in the battle. Obviously, a fixed prison was impossible. So a tiger cage was used. This was a small portable prison which could be moved quickly when necessary. It was constructed from bamboo sticks and was approximately five feet square. It was too small for the average American to stretch out or to stand up. Anyone confined to a tiger cage was cramped and extremely uncomfortable. One P.O.W. said he was kept in a tiger cage for six years!

As I listened to the description of the tiger cage, I thought of the many who have created their own private "tiger cage." They are not P.O.W.'s; they are P.O.T.'s (Prisoners of Thought). Wherever they go their portable prison goes with them. They are caught in the prison of their negative habits and attitudes. They have either locked themselves in or have allowed their friends, families, or associates to gradually build a "cage" around their lives. The bars of fear, embarrassment, tradition, social pressure, evil habits, or playing-it-safe, are all part of the bars which have kept them locked in their prison.

The tragedy of this type of "cage" is that it is portable. You take it wherever you go. You can change jobs, relocate, re-marry, and still be trapped in your own tiger cage. You are locked in.

If you are a P.O.T. locked in a tiger cage, you need to sit down now and examine each of the bars, one at a time. Consider why they are there. Look at each bar closely. All of them can be removed. If they were put in the cage, they can be taken out of the cage. Begin now to take them out, one at a time. You can remove the bars through faith, prayer, and determination. You will discover that when one bar is removed all the rest seem to connect and come out more easily.

Let Christ hand you the secret of liberation. He said, "If the Son therefore shall make you free, ye shall be free indeed" (John 8:36). I challenge you today to begin to disassemble your "tiger cage."

5

PERSISTENCE–
THE ONE WAY
TO SUCCEED

God, is it true a person can
have everything, and yet
be a failure?
Then what is success?
What is this basic desire
and drive which causes me to go on,
to go after the things which
I need?
Persistence! It must be a
divine spark which keeps
the human race
in the race!
Amen.

PERSISTENCE—THE ONE WAY TO SUCCEED

Educators seek to instill at least three things into their students: knowledge, good judgement, and persistence. And of the three, persistence is the key which unlocks the doors to knowledge and good judgement.

Many people have succeeded without formal education. Some have even succeeded without using good judgement! But no one has gone anywhere worth going without persistence. At the base of all accomplishment is persistence, desire, and determination. Show me a person with these qualities and I will show you a successful person. Persistence grows out of desire.

Jesus said, "Whatever ye desire . . . " (Mark 11:24). Whatever you *desire*, Jesus was saying, will be what you *receive.* Power in prayer is based on desire, and desire leads to persistence.

Nothing in the world can take the place of persistence. The best training, the best talent, and even the best opportunity will not take the place of persistence.

St. Paul said, "I press toward the mark . . . " (Philippians 3:14). This was the drive of his life pressing on to know, to gain, to achieve. This persistent goal was the greatest force in the heart of the apostle.

How do you develop persistence? What is the one basic element in being persistent?

The essential ingredient is a longing for something more than what you have. It is the empty heart that longs to be filled. It is the invalid who longs for strength. The poverty-stricken who longs for wealth. It is the sinner who searches for forgiveness. The guilty cry for pardon!

Whatever you fervently desire and persistently seek in life is waiting just for the taking. All of your desires can be fulfilled. You can succeed if you develop the quality of persistence in your life.

6

WHAT'S IN CONTROL?

Lord, why do I put so many days
on the scrap pile?
I lose control . . .
because I fail to keep
a single purpose.
So . . .
tomorrow I'll try again
. . . for it will be a new beginning.
THANKS!
Amen.

WHAT'S IN CONTROL?

Are you a slave to circumstances? Do you ever feel that everything in your life is out of control? Whatever gets your attention will eventually get you.

Have you ever gotten up in the morning with a bright countenance, motivated for the day, and then a foreboding thought, like a slowly-moving shadow, began to creep into your mind? Little by little that dark thought gained momentum until it had your full attention! Your bright countenance went into hiding and defeat and gloom took its place. You were out of control. By noon the day seemed lost and you were divided from your earlier interest and intent. The sun had set at noon, for another day was wasted. You put that day on the scrap pile.

The Bible says, "A double minded man is unstable in all his ways" (James 1:8). When the mind is divided, goals are confused, effort is cut in half, and results are low.

But there is a power, an inner ability, which can help you master your emotions and bring discipline to your world. Your future is bright as you allow the power of God to direct you. "In all thy ways acknowledge him, and he shall direct thy paths," we are told (Proverbs 3:6). What you are, what you do a year from now, depends wholly on who or what you allow to control your mind and life today. If He directs your paths and helps you control your mind, nothing will be impossible in life.

Orison Swett Marven puts it in these words, "The majority of failures in life are simply the victims of their mental defeats. Their conviction that they cannot succeed as others do robs them of vigor and determination which self-confidence imparts, and they don't even half try to succeed." If this is the situation in your life, you can change the negative image which has you in control. You can be a winner mentally which, in return, will make you a winner in reality.

St. Paul says in I Timothy 4:15-16, "Meditate upon these things; give thyself wholly to them; that thy profiting may appear to all. Take heed unto thyself, and unto the doctrine; continue in them: for in doing this thou shalt both save thyself, and them that hear thee."

7

LOOK AS IF
YOU HAVE
SUCCEEDED

Is it really true . . .
I can have what I
believe
and desire...
If I pray.
Sounds good! But,
who backs up this hope of mine?
CHRIST!
Then I'll look like I have it . . .
And I will!
Amen.

LOOK AS IF YOU HAVE SUCCEEDED

A young man asked a very successful banker what suggestions he had for someone who wanted to succeed. The banker replied, "Look as though you have already succeeded." Shakespeare said, "Assume a virtue if you have it not."

Look the part. Be successful in your own heart. Let "faith seeds" be planted, cultivated and start to grow in the ground of your hopes.

Jesus said, "...what things so ever ye desire, when ye pray, believe that ye receive them, and ye shall have them" (Mark 11:24). He stated that you must act as if the prayer has been heard and answered long before you actually receive, or realize, the answer.

Your countenance, the sparkle of your eye, and the tone of your voice all shine like a bright light in the darkness when you believe.

But you must decide what to believe and what you desire. Make it clear to your own heart and subconscious mind exactly what you want. "Keep thy heart with all diligence; for out of it are the issues of life," we are told (Proverbs 4:23). Plan your desires in detail as much as you can. Then act as though you were already successful in the area in which you want to succeed.

I presented the idea of a "treasure map" to my church. I went through many different magazines and clipped pictures, titles, and words which depicted my success desires. My daughter and I glued these on a large poster board. The collage of pictures, words, and concepts were in all sizes and shapes. As I preached on "Faith Can Achieve Anything" I displayed the poster and said, "Why not make your own treasure map and then write a letter to God each day and put it in a 'God Box' thanking Him in advance for those things which you desire." My wife went home and immediately constructed herself a little "God Box." Each day (or oftener if the occasion arises) she writes a short letter or note to God and drops it in her "God Box."

"Does it work?" you ask. Ask her and she will say without hesitation, "Yes!"

Every time you desire to achieve a certain goal act on it. If it does not harm another and is to the glory of God, then make your plans in advance for receiving it, for you will surely receive it sooner or later. " . . . It is your Father's good pleasure to give you the Kingdom," Jesus said (Luke 12:32).

A mysterious law is set in motion by faith when you act on your success instincts. Act and speak as if you have already received all you desire from God's storehouses. Make your desires real in your mind by prayer based on the promises of God. You will soon find them to be a reality in your life!

8

THINK YOUR
OBSTACLES INTO
OPPORTUNITIES

Father, why the obstacles?
Is it true
my thinking affects the obstacles?
But how?
I suppose what I think is what I pray
And prayer can turn obstacles
into opportunities . . .
If I believe.
I BELIEVE!
Amen.

THINK YOUR OBSTACLES INTO OPPORTUNITIES

St. Paul said, "...whatsoever things are true...honest...just ... pure ... lovely ... of good report; if there be any virtue ... any praise, think on these things." (Philippians 4:8).

What about your thinking? Does your mind drift to low, gloomy, and depressing thoughts, or are you filled with happy thoughts? Do you feed your mind with worthwhile material day by day? Do you feed your subconscious mind strong, vigorous, and successful thoughts? Whatever you center your thoughts on will reveal itself eventually!

The successful person and the unsuccessful person differ only in how they think and act. The unsuccessful person sees *obstacles*, not opportunities, while the successful person sees *opportunities in the obstacles*. One sees the opportunity and seizes it, the other sees only the obstacle and flees from it. One moves out of faith while the other freezes out of fear. One stands looking and hoping while the other, with a bolder spirit, dashes by and receives the reward.

Out of the mind of God comes good, unlimited, strong, and vigorous thoughts. A wealth of love for you, beyond human conception, is in the mind of God. "...in Him is no darkness at all" (I John 1:5). God wills for you the best!

Sometimes I think God must look down at man and wonder, "Man, why all this mess?" We create our own mess by the way we think, act, and react.

How successful do you want to be? How full of God's life, vitality, and accomplishments do you want to be? What you think about, day after day, will eventually be produced in your life. Your driving thought will become a reality.

What you will become in the tomorrows lies within your own heart and mind today. God has not put a limitation on your

41

achievements! If there are any limitations they come from thinking you cannot achieve. Become what you are capable of becoming. Watch what you think; the seeds you sow will grow into a harvest.

9

DON'T LOOK
AT WHAT
YOU SEE

Lord, I think I'm looking
at the limitations.
Struggling to free myself.
Odds are not to be considered...
So, I'll look away from them
to Thee.
Let all odds stand there!
I believe we can, Lord!
Amen.

DON'T LOOK AT WHAT YOU SEE

Five thousand hungry men, far from food, sat waiting in a desert to be fed. Judging by appearances only, five barley loaves was hardly enough to feed them. One loaf to a thousand men seemed utterly impossible. Looking at the odds, it seemed hopeless!

Have you ever asked yourself these questions as you stood looking at your five little loaves? "Why do I always have to face the avalanche of debt and limitation?" "Must I always struggle against great odds?" "When will I have what I need?"

A thousand to one seems impossible. Why even consider the possibility of something becoming better than it is? And so we fail because, after you and I have drawn from the best of human understanding, reasoning, and wisdom in these circumstances, we usually abide by the results—it's impossible.

The great law of liberation in your situation is: "Judge not according to the appearance . . . " (John 7:24). Don't look at what you see! Don't judge your potential by the resources of the moment! This is not closing your eyes to reality or putting your head in the sand; it is placing your attention on the invisible source of all things. The All-Spirit, the All-Substance, the All-Creator, is at hand—Christ the Lord!

If you have a pressing need, you also have a pressing supply; one calls for the other.

Let your mind melt into the infinite God from whom all things come. He is the prime cause and the prime mover in your universe.

You have the seed of confidence which, when planted, contains the potential of growth. The invisible forces of nature start to work on the seed the minute it is planted. You plant the seed, and the process begins to produce the desired results. It is a natural, simple, and normal process. Now you wait for the results. Why should you consider the producing of substance any more difficult than the producing of fruit from the seed in the soil?

Let your substance be natural and normal. "Don't judge from appearances!" Look at your situation with eyes of faith. Let your pressing need turn your eyes to the abundant supply which is pressing through to meet your need.

10

WATCH OUT
FOR EXCESSIVE
CAREFULNESS

It seemes the harder I try
the more difficult it becomes.
Why, Lord?
Being so careful to do the
right thing,
I stumble into the wrong.
I am discovering . . .
I can depend on the freedom
in Christ
to be
and to do
what is best for You
and for me.
This is effortless . . . but fruitful!
Amen.

WATCH OUT FOR EXCESSIVE CAREFULNESS

Have you ever walked a plank? If the board were on the ground, you could walk across without faltering. You would not be overly careful about staying on the plank because you know there would be no danger if you fell off. But, take that same narrow piece of wood and put it 100 feet in the air and then attempt to walk over it! Your excessive carefulness coupled with the fear of falling, would cause you to be unsteady and unsure. This excessive, negative feedback would cause you to be awkward and incapable, full of fear and trembling. Your over-concerned attitude could cause stumbling and death.

With the plank up in the air you have a greater purpose for not wanting to fall off, and this very purpose may cause you to stumble. It is called, "purpose tremor," in medical terms. It always happens when you try too hard.

Anxiety is a form of excessive carefulness. It is wanting to achieve so hard that it paralyzes, making achievement virtually impossible; it is trying to do so well that you can't do well at all. When you over-manage yourself, attempting to avoid one mistake, you create a hundred more. Excessive correction leads to greater mistakes, frustrations, and failures.

When you are too careful the result is failure or awkwardness. The excessive feedback of negative thoughts causes certain failure. Your mind is telling you to be careful, don't do that, watch out for this, or you might fall.

The negative approach tells you what *not* to do. You become so taken up with negative feedback and inhibitions that, as a result, you never learn to live freely and creatively. You lack zest and spontaneity toward God and life. You become so filled with carefulness that your image becomes one of inhibition. You are careful that you *not* make a mistake, that you *not* go to certain places. You feel you are *not* doing enough, *not* praying enough, *not* witnessing enough. And you become so caught up in the "nots" that you actually cut off your life from a full and free fellowship with Christ. Life becomes awkward, ingrown and in spite of all efforts, ends up fruitless. You still miss the mark. The result of excessive negativism is deterioration of performance.

Someone said, "I don't like these cold, precise, perfect people, who, in order not to speak wrong, don't speak at all and, in order not to do wrong, never do anything."

Good news! Jesus has come to set you free. "...where the Spirit of the Lord is, there is liberty" (II Corinthians 3:17).

11

THERE IS POWER
IN THE POISE
OF PEACE

I bless the Lord for the
peace He gives.
Peace brings poise . . .
control in the midst
of trouble.
There will still be uncontrollable
situations but never
an uncontrolled reaction.
—If I have Your peace,
poise is the evidence!
Amen.

THERE IS POWER IN THE POISE OF PEACE

Do you have poise in strange and new situations? Or are you forever trying to please people, hoping to gain their approval? Do you consciously seek to impress others, only to find that you lose your poise at the critical moment.

The way to make a good impression is to simply *not try* to make an impression. Don't even stop to consider whether you are making a good impression on people.

Jesus said, " . . . my peace I give unto you . . ." (John 14:27). His peace brings poise. His peace contains power, sustaining you in the hour you face the unknown. With His peace you are ready for anything life may ask of you. If you have His peace and poise you will always make a good impression. Don't try, just accept the fact!

Jesus always had *things* under control because *he* was under control. In His Spirit He was calm and collected. Even while dying on the cross Jesus had poise and could say, "into thy hands I commend my spirit..." (Luke 23: 46).

James Mangan defined poise as *immunity*. He says, "This attitude of being immune to strangers, or strange situations, this total disregard for all the unknown or unexpected has a name; it is called poise. Poise is the deliberate shunting of all fears arising from new and uncontrollable circumstances." You must learn the secret of immunity if you want to succeed easily; become immune to strangers, strange situations and new experiences.

To have the peace of poise which Christ gives, shove aside your fears that arise from new and uncontrollable circumstances. Turn your eyes from what might go wrong and begin to think and pray only for what might go right. Keep your mind focused on the things you *do* want, not on the things you *don't* want. If you don't want fear, center your mind on peace. If you don't want failure, keep your mind on success. We are told, "Thou wilt

53

keep him in perfect peace, whose mind is stayed on thee . . . ."
(Isaiah 26:3). And, "Casting all your care upon Him; for He
careth for you" (I Peter 5:7).

You can create obstacles by thinking about them. Worry about an
obstacle and you will usually be hindered by that barrier. The only
way to unlock your true self is through poise and self-confidence;
through knowing that what you are is good to the very core of your
being. You defeat only yourself when you think it's wrong to be
right about your ideas, your opinions and your aspirations. Learn to
stand tall, walk humbly with your God, and take leadership for His
glory.

The poise which Christ gives is also the poise of power. It
disintegrates the inhibitions of your life. When you have poise,
the fear of being wrong or out of control will be replaced by the
faith of acceptance and ability. Christ has come to set you free.
Let Him give you immunity to all things, except Himself.

12

EVERYTHING
AFTER ITS KIND

I don't understand seed time
and harvest . . . but I know
it works.
Father, is this true in the
spiritual world as well . . .
and financial?
What I sow
I reap.
This is good news!
Now I can regulate what I
get out of life by what I
give to life.
It really comes back in greater quanities.
The returns are unbelievable . . .
GREAT!
Amen.

EVERYTHING AFTER ITS KIND

Do you recall the old-fashioned hand pumps on the farm? To start the water flowing you had to prime the pump by pouring in a little water. In order to create a vacuum (which would produce the needed supply of water from the pump) you had to *give* up some water so you could *receive* more water. You had to be willing to let go of some of the very substance you needed.

One of the great principles in the Bible is: Everything reproduces after its kind. You read in the first chapter of Genesis how God made everything to reproduce after its kind. Gen.

Everything in the world works on this principle of planting and reaping. You will always have to pay the price of giving a little of what you have in order to reap the harvest of what you really need. You must sow, plant, and give away the very things you need so that it can reproduce itself in your own life.

Do you need friends? Sow seeds of friendliness. Do you need faith? Use the faith you have. If you need money, give some. Give it freely, cheerfully; give it as unto the Lord. With every pressing need there is a pressing supply.

The Bible says, "There is (he) that scattereth, and yet increaseth; and there is (he) that withholdeth more than is meet, but it tendeth to poverty" (Proverbs 11:24).

Again the Bible says, "The liberal soul shall be made fat: and he that watereth shall be watered also himself." (Proverbs 11:25).

All unselfish energy, all blessings (as well as cursings) return to you in greater quantity. You get back more than you give, both good and bad. All giving is an outward flow of energy which compels a return. There is a cycle of giving and returning which cannot be altered. There is no act which does not return itself manifold.

You must prepare for your returns. Dig your ditches and prepare for the floods. Plant your vineyards, accept the gifts of God. Affirm the truth that you expect to reap "...after its kind." Sow the seeds of money and claim riches. Plant the seeds of encouragement and claim happiness. Don't let your mind dwell on despair and discouragement for if you do you will reap exactly its kind. Keep your mind on the full, unlimited supply of God. Act as though you have already received what you have been sowing!

13

FAILURES
WON'T DO IT

You know, Lord, it's
strange why so few
really try to succeed.
To be in the failure class
is embarrassing.
Many times wanting not to make
a mistake
I do nothing . . . and then
find out later I really made
a mistake!

I'll do it!
Amen.

FAILURES WON'T DO IT

Have you ever wondered what makes a person successful? Why does one person succeed and another person in the same situation fail? Two people can be in the same business, have similar backgrounds, enjoy the same type of training, and yet one is outstanding while the other fades into failure. What makes the difference?

What is it that failure-people *won't do*? What is it that success-people *always do*? Is it going the second mile as opposed to doing only what is required? Is it that one has pleasure in what he is doing while the other only puts in his time? To the one, all work is hard, time consuming and difficult; but to the other work is fun and time off is boring.

Now, I think everyone needs time away from his work, to get away from the pressure and rest. But I wonder if failure-people are looking to get away from it all more than they are looking to succeed. Someone suggested that if you want to succeed you should make your work fun and then take your fun seriously!

Success is achieved by only a small number of people. That always amazes me. There are only a minority of homes that are happy, a small group of husbands and wives who still enjoy each other after 20 years of married life. Only a handful of churches, homes, and organizations enjoy growth and fulfillment.

Why? I think it's because success is really unnatural; unnatural in that it takes *super-natural* confidence and ability to make it happen. Successful people, leaders, organizations, or homes are scarce because they require more time, dedication and energy to create and maintain. One must sacrifice the right to oneself in order to excel.

I made a little diagram the other day. This diagram is set up on a curve from 0 - 100%. I estimated that the minority of the people are at opposite ends; that is, 10% of the people are failures and 10% of the people are high achievers. The other 80% are in the gray matter in between. They live in the majority category. The world seldom takes notice of the 80% because they are like trees in the forest. The 10% that are succeeders stand out like a burning bush on a lonely desert. They are seen and known, either pitied or envied.

Which category are you in? Failures will not form the habit of reaching for results. Successful-minded people will. One seeks only to get by, while the other strives for excellence. Success is achieved by extraordinary efforts and methods. Find out what failures won't do and then *do it!* This is the secret of maintaining success.

14

YOU ARE
WHAT YOU THINK

Lord, I believe that
what I think is what I do . . .
what I'll become, too.
I fix my mind to think Your thoughts . . .
thoughts of You I find
in the Bible.
I reaffirm thinking up . . .
thinking good,
positive thoughts
which have hope in them.
I will think of ways to grow,
achieve,
and enjoy.
What I think today
I will become
and do
someday.
Amen.

YOU ARE WHAT YOU THINK

Your mind dwells on the things it loves. Jesus said, "Where your treasure is, there will your heart be also" (Matthew 6:21).

Sir Isaac Newton was asked how he discovered the low of gravity. He quietly replied, "By thinking about it all the time."

Each of us becomes what we think. We will most likely do, or become, whatever we think about the most. We rise or fall to the level of our thoughts. This is the reason we have happy people and sad people, bums and saints, millionaires and poverty-stricken people—because of what they think.

Tell me what you think and I can tell you what you will become. Be careful what you think about, for it will surely come into your life. Think about the things that you want, not about the things you don't want.

Thoughts are like any other habit. They can be created and cultivated. You can become accustomed to feeling better or bitter each day. Many people fight life. Is it any wonder their world is full of troubles, setbacks, and difficulties?

It can be natural, though, to love, trust and expect the good. How happy and freewheeling your world could become if you would develop the habit of expecting the good, looking for the best, and speaking to all people as if they were really important to you. Consciously—but more likely unconsciously—you are creating and sculpturing your own personal world. There isn't anyone who can force you into his world. Your world is the place only you can make.

Paul says, " . . . for I have learned, in whatsoever state I am, therewith to be content" (Philippians 4:11). That is to say, I am learning to be contented with what and where I am for this moment. Paul stated that he could be up or down, full or empty, and still be content. He had inner control. His secret of living a successful life was within.

You can become so fixed, so bent on going in the path of progress, that nothing except the will of God can deter you. Your inner control is what keeps you on the path of progress. Your thought life becomes an architectural drawing for your life. It is the constant thought, focused on the purpose of your life, which will at last bring you to your desired goal. You will build your world to the exact specifications of the thoughts you have designed on the architectural drawing boards of your mind.

15

FORGIVENESS
AND FORTUNE

When I forgive,
it seems best to
forget, also.
I guess that forgetting is the key
to forgiving
You know, Lord, I feel better, too.
When I feel better,
I do better
And when I do better
my fortunes grow.
I wonder if all these are tied together.
If so, here goes
. . . I forgive
. . . I forget
Look at the future of joy,
peace
good feelings
plenty.
It's all tied to forgiving . . .
and forgetting.
Amen.

FORGIVENESS AND FORTUNE

Forgiveness is tied to forgetting, which leads to fortune—a fortune that may come in many different packages.

Who really gets hurt in unforgiveness? Have you ever thought of forgiveness as a road to better health? If you are holding some old, unforgiving attitude in your heart it could lead you to misfortune, heartache, or even death.

It is my conviction that forgiveness and the best life has to offer are closely tied together. When I relate forgiveness with fortune, I speak of more than money or possessions. There are many people who seemingly have everything in life but lack the fortunes of peace, love and good health.

The Bible says, "Be still, and know that I am God...." (Psalm 46:10). Get quiet. Come apart from your world and sit before the Lord. Let Him examine your needs, attitudes and feelings; there may be a spot of disease in your love or attitude that needs healing.

If you will sit before the Lord and let go of all unforgiveness you will discover peace and happiness flooding your soul. Good things will begin to happen in your life. You will experience healing!

To experience healing you must first determine if there is an attitude of unforgiveness within you. If you are involved in the spirit of criticism, whether it be talk or attitude, you need to ask God to forgive you. If possible, ask the person involved to forgive you. Try looking upon those people with eyes of love. See them not as enemies but as people who need love and understanding.

Perhaps you have found yourself part of a critical group, and have even felt holy in "defending" the gospel, or you have taken pride in cutting another person down. All this may have been done behind the mask of "religious concern," but it's of the devil! This kind of attitude will kill your love, deaden your faith, and stop the wheels of success in your life.

You may have had a disagreement with another. You may have been hurt. But if you cling to unforgiveness, old grudges, or criticisms, you are only feeding the fires of self-destruction.

Forgiveness brings fortune in many packages. Jesus says, "When ye stand praying, forgive . . . ." (Mark 11:25).

Say now, "I release my feelings of unforgiveness toward anyone, anywhere." Now watch for the package of fortune which will come to you. It's amazing how the package of fortune knows the address of the forgiving person.

16

THE POWER OF

SYNERGISM

You know, Lord, it's hard to achieve alone.
Is this why You said,
"If two shall agree . . . ."?
Togetherness is toughness.
There must be one person
who will agree with me . . .
and I with them.
Agreeing is like music . . . it's a melody
with each person playing a different note
but not a different key.
All life's duties are the notes,
Lord,
when we play in your key,
that's harmony!
Amen!

THE POWER OF SYNERGISM

"What in the world is synergism?"

This was my reaction too when I first heard the word. Synergism means two or more discreet people join in action, thereby creating a greater effect than if they acted separately. Synergism, then, means that when two join together they discover greater power than they would alone.

In the light of the Scriptures one can chase a thousand, and two can put ten thousand to flight. (See Deuteronomy 32:30.)

Synergism is explained in the words of Jesus when He says, " . . . if two of you shall agree . . . ." (Matthew 18:19). And again, " . . . where two or three are gathered together in my name, there am I . . . . " (Matthew 18:20). There is much in the Bible about synergism; " . . . if a house be divided against itself, that house cannot stand." (Mark 3:25) And in the book of Acts, " . . . they were all with one accord in one place" (Acts 2:1).

The effects of joint action by people with one great purpose is unlimited. It is almost impossible to stop that force once it is set into motion. The power that is created by the unity of minds is almost beyond human comprehension.

The great purpose of the Holy Spirit in the church is to unite people in order to make the church indestructible.

If a home has the power of synergism it becomes a wall of protection to all its members, and there isn't anything it can't accomplish. Jesus sent the disciples ahead of Him two by two. Why? Because He understood this law of synergism. He also gathered twelve men around him, knowing the power of this law in their lives as well as His own. When two or more minds, wills or affections are wholly set on one thing, there is very little chance of that one thing ever going wrong or not being fully accomplished.

Great minds send forth great thoughts which incessantly draw great events. It always amazes me when the very things I have been praying for, thinking about, and expecting actually show up. But, I shouldn't be amazed, for this is the law of synergism.

If two of you will center your attention steadily and deliberately on the desired results, you will feel no need to argue, beg, plead, or appeal to anyone for your desired good. You can know in your heart the source of the power that is bringing what you need and is making you what you are. The power of synergism is open to you who will come together discreetly for an all-consuming purpose. It works!

Find a prayer partner, a faith partner, and unite your common goals. Then watch the universe turn itself inside out to enable you to reach your desired objectives because of the power of synergism.

17

PROSPERITY
IS FOR YOU

Lord, I have heard it is wrong
to prosper
and yet

it seems everyone
seeks to prosper?
What is prosperity?
Is it money?
Is it a good family?
Is it self-worth?
…maybe all three…
You promised prosperity!
So…whatever You know it to be
let it be in me
and for me!
Amen.

PROSPERITY IS FOR YOU

It is positively right for you to prosper!

Russell H. Conwell said, "You have no right to be poor." Prosperity means you are receiving favorable results. You are supposed to live a full, abundant, and favorable life even though people do not believe it is right for them to flourish.

There is a life which is full, rich, and totally satisfying. Speaking of the blessed or happy man, the Bible says, "...and whatsoever he doeth shall prosper" (Psalm 1:3). This is a promise just as much as John 3:16 when it says, "For God so loved the world, that he gave his only begotten Son, that *whosoever* believeth in him should not perish, but have everlasting life."

Many of us do not accept this truth concerning prosperity. We act as if we are opposed to the experience of the abundant life. We must realize that the Lord is concerned with the total man: the mind, the soul, and the body. It was the prayer of St. Paul that you would be sanctified in all three areas. God wants your life to be blessed and set apart for His glory and the good of your world. He wants to help you solve your spiritual, personal, and economic problem.

Some of you have a conflict between prosperity and piety. You don't accept the fact that whatever you do will prosper; therefore, nothing ever seems to go right for you.

Some of you may think it is the will of God for you to fail, to be miserable, poor, and to suffer lack. The question to settle in your mind is whether poverty is a spiritual virtue or a common vice! This conflict will erect a barrier between you and the big life Christ came to give. No matter how hard you work, or seek to succeed, you will shut the gates to all the unlimited resources of Heaven if you fail to believe prosperity is the will of God for you.

Lack in any form is a limitation. Look at lack as a signpost pointing to supply. All lack calls to be filled; every vacuum hungers to be filled. If you don't like your level of prosperity, you are the one who must change. Repent, stop looking at God as stingy and one who withholds the good from you—He is willing to give you the Kingdom.

Now put movement into your desire. Busy your hands in a thousand ways with something worthwhile for your world. The greater the number of hands you have working in a worthwhile cause the greater your chances of having prosperity returned to you. You may write a book, give something to the world which benefits the human race and you will be surprised with the returns.

There are many people living in poverty and misery because they missed the truth of giving something first. Learn to love all, to give to everyone, and withhold nothing good from those who need it. If you are choosy as to when and to whom you give, you cancel out the law of prosperity.

Love all—give to all—make every act as great as you can. You will enjoy favorable and flourishing results which add up to prosperity!

18

RADIATION
CREATES
ATTRACTION

Jesus is the light of the world.
He said I am also
the light of the world.
He is radiating through me . . .
and, all light attracts,
so, I must be attractive.
But, what I attract
is what I radiate.
Lord, adjust my radiation to be real,
encouraging to others
and succeeding!
No one wants to be
a fading light
. . . I don't think so . . .
Not me, anyway!
Amen.

RADIATION CREATES ATTRACTION

Do you radiate? Do people pick up your radiation? If so, what kind of vibrations do you radiate in your world?

Radiation is nothing more than the real you. It's the atmosphere you create, the color of the personality you project, and the tone of your voice. Radiation is the vibration of your thoughts and your deep inner-self coming through to others. Radiation is what you really are at a particular given moment.

Great hearts send forth great wave lengths of radiation. Small hearts and little minds send forth weak and limited thought radiations.

The point to remember is that we attract whatever we radiate. What we radiate we shall receive in return. Jesus says, "Ye are the light of the world . . . . " (Matthew 5:14). It is foolish for you to curse the darkness, just turn on the light! Paul emphasized this when he said, "To the one we are the savor of death unto death; and to the other the savor of life unto life...." (II Corinthians 2:16).

There are people who say, "Everything happens to me." "I can't win for losing." "This is a hard, old world." "I am never lucky." "Why don't things ever go right for me?" All of these radiations of failure, lack, and limitation will draw those very things back to you. Perhaps you have said, "This is going to be a rough day," and sure enough, it was!

Most people who are living below what they want actually do so because they really *want* to live there. The effort involved in change is too great; the path of least resistance is easier. They ask the question, "Why put up the struggle?" and quit. Many would like to have the worm, but they don't want to pay the price to be the early bird. And you can't get something for nothing.

You can have the best of everything when you give full measure for the good that you want to receive. Doug Oldham once said, while singing for us in a TV rally, "Let's give them their money's worth tonight." This is the attitude which attracts success. You draw your supply from the limitless resources of God if you radiate a full measure and act upon worthy deeds to the benefit of this world.

It is a law of the universe that you will attract what you radiate. The only thing you ever attracted without effort was the mercy of God. You can only come to God as the Spirit draws you. If left to ourselves we would surely perish. But your need attracted His supply; your sin attracted His forgiveness.

But in every other area of life you will attract what you radiate—no more and no less.

19

THE SEED
OF INCREASE

I want to increase what I have
because I will increase
what I am.
The greater I increase my talents,
the greater my talents
Increase my cash and character,
for cash flow without character would
end in disgrace.
Father, I will create . . . not compete
I will invest . . . not envy
I will become . . . to have and to share.

Where do I begin?
Amen.

THE SEED OF INCREASE

"And unto one he gave five talents, to another two, and to another one; to every man according to his ability..." (Matthew 25:15).

Increase, growth, and gain are vital parts of the human race; all the universe is reaching for them. Everything in the world is pushing toward some type of increase or growth. It is a basic need in all of us to desire more, to be seeking increase and growth. We seek to increase our joy, love, faith, and money. We seek to increase the glory of God in the earth.

scriptural. Jesus told the parable of the talents which were given to several men. One had been given one talent, another two, and another five. An increase was expected from each. All of them made an increase from the "seed talent" except one. Those that had an increase were commended by the Lord, the one who failed to plant the seed of increase was condemned.

Seek to plant the seed of increase in every area of your life. You can enjoy great increase and growth without hurting or harming anyone else. In fact, you will enrich the well-being of others, making their lives more productive and planting seeds of growth in your own life at the same time.

The unconcerned heart and the uninformed mind believe you can only get ahead in the world at the expense of someone else. This is a fatal mistake! You cannot enrich the lives of others without enriching your own life. It is equally true that you cannot hurt another without hurting yourself.

As you plant the seed of increase do not seek to compete. The competitor is usually an imitator, a "me too" individual. The big difference between the competitor and the creator is that one competes solely for the sake of competition, missing the thrill of creativity, while the other simply seeks to create. One competes, the other creates. The creative person adds value to all he is associated with. He benefits more people and stays ahead of competitors for the "me too" people are usually a step behind the creative individual.

You can create a tidal wave of blessing for the future if you will understand the law of creativity in all you do. Sow the seed of increase today and watch a harvest come in tomorrow.

"Whatsoever a man soweth, that shall he also reap" (Galatians 6:7).

20

CREATIVE

LIMITATIONS

You know, Lord,
I blamed my limitations for my lack
but what I failed to see was
my limitations should have been
my assets.
I never knew limitations could provide motivation.
If what I want to do has roadblocks
help me to build another road.
I will thank You, Father,
for these infirmities.
I turn all my limitations to assets . . .
starting now!
Amen.

CREATIVE LIMITATIONS

Frank Lloyd Wright, the great architect, said, "The human race was built most nobly when limitations were greatest and, therefore, when most was required of the imagination in order to build at all." He goes on to say, "Limitations seem to have always been best friends of the architect."

The Apostle Paul expressed this same idea: "...Most gladly, therefore will I rather glory in my infirmities, that the power of Christ may rest upon me" (II Corinthians 12:9).

Your limitations can become launching pads for creative living. The pain of places, people, and problems are friends in disguise; friends that can enable you to build a greater life of service and personal reward.

A highly successful businessman said to me one day, "I never had a college degree as some of the other men with whom I worked. Knowing this limitation, I worked harder. I became more creative and spent more time than the rest at what I was doing. This attitude finally put me in the lead and at the top of my field." His limitation pushed him into creative living.

Find your own unique talents and abilities. Accept your individuality. Realize that in this creative manner no other person in the world functions exactly as you do. Develop your capacity to pray and live creatively. Determine the effectiveness of ideas you have created recently. Analyze how you are improving your mind and your imagination. Are you using your limitations as a motivation for creative excellence?

I recall some of the limitations in the early years of my training. When I was a boy, my family moved many times in the city of Louisville, Kentucky, and it was common for us children to skip school for days on end. I failed the second grade. Education and learning were not priorities in my family until my

Dad was converted to Jesus Christ.

In later years when I started Bible School, my grades came hard that first year. But, knowing my limitations, I did not get into competition with the others. I practiced creative praying and thinking. I determined to succeed by the grace of God — and I did!

Learn to use your limitations; they are the best spurs in life. When you create new concepts you are paving the road to success, not only for yourself but for multitudes who will follow you in your generation and in the generations to come.

21

THE HABIT OF
GOOD HABITS

I guess a habit is doing something
without thinking;
it's almost an unconscious reaction.
Lord, work on my reactions!
I'll help...by correction,
creation
and control.
It should be rewarding.
I feel the change starting...
NOW!
Amen.

THE HABIT OF GOOD HABITS

A good habit is like a good friend, it's always there in times of stress. Forming good habits is like making many friends. The more friends you have the greater your chances for protection, being loved, and abundant living. Life is exciting to the person who has good friends, but it can become frustrating to the person who has "unfriendly friends." Habits work the same way.

It is easy to acquire bad habits, it takes little effort. Bad habits seem to come more easily than good ones. And the elimination of bad habits takes more time and effort than the elimination of a good habit. Habits can be either the best of servants or the worst of masters.

The Bible tells us one fruit of the Spirit is "temperance," or self-control. If your habits become your master, you no longer have yourself under control. Losing self-control can itself become a habit, and once you have lost self-control you have lost the ability to create good habits.

You can form the habit of being gloomy, depressed, and miserable. This habit can even become like an old hat—you feel better when it's on your head. There are many who live in a depression brought on by their thought habits. They eventually believe this is a part of their personality and the best they can achieve. They have clothed themselves with a concept which accepts a bad attitude as a way of life. These people are never at peace unless they are at war; they are never comfortable unless they are uncomfortable.

Remember, you are the creator of your own world. Form good habits such as: praising the Lord every day, waiting on God brings peace. The habit of speaking well of others brings a return of friends. The habits of Godly thinking, hoping, trusting, and creative living bring plentiful rewards. All of these make for great joy in living and great reward for the effort you made to form good habits.

Keep good habits alive with devotion and dedication. Let your habits be more than a master. Let them be a joyful way of life.

Even the best of habits can become stagnant. Keep them alive by regular inspections and frequent dedication of your ways to the Lord. Watch what you weave, for tomorrow they will form your pattern of living.

"But the fruit of the Spirit is love, joy, peace, longsuffering, gentleness, goodness, faith, meekness, self-control . . . . " (Galatians 5:22-23).

22

THE FEARFULNESS

OF FEAR

Lord, fear has kept me back
more than any other force.
I fear people . . . new places
opportunities . . . new ways
And mostly . . .
a new self-image.
I feel too comfortable in the path of safety.
But I know I really cheat myself
when I let fear rule me.
NO MORE?
I renounce fear right now!
Amen.

THE FEARFULNESS OF FEAR

Emerson wrote, "A determined man, by his very attitude and the tone of his voice, puts a stop to defeat and begins to conquer." The opposite of fear is courage. It is the anxiety of fear which causes most opportunities to be lost and courage never to be born.

One of the great secrets in overcoming fear is to face it with faith and conquer it through action. Moving ahead, even against fear, brings hope and creates courage. You always rule out the possibility of winning by refusing to risk defeat in the face of fear. You can reach anything desirable if you will risk the possibility of defeat. But, if you do nothing because of fear, you are sure to be defeated and lose altogether.

Even the most desirable things look impossible until you conquer the feeling of fear and make an initial attempt, no matter how feeble your attempt may be. There is a good possibility the next move will be the winning one.

No doubt you have made hundreds of moves. Perhaps all of them were unproductive; not one has paid off yet. But keep on, for each move which does not pay off is another you know will *not* work. And you are conquering the fearfulness of fear and ignorance.

You will improve your feelings of self-worth each time you make an attempt to overcome the fearfulness of fear. It's the thousand attempts (as you conquer fear) which will draw to you the very possibility of accomplishing your desired project. So, meet your fears head on. The longer you wait the harder it will become to tackle your fear.

You can cheat yourself out of what you want, the things you need, and those things you desire to accomplish in life because you are afraid to try, to seek, and to ask. If you know the laws of

God and His universe, you will try and keep on trying, for lack of courage guarantees failure. So, do not accept your lack of courage. Act in confidence on your desires.

The fearfulness of fear carries its own defeat. You may be surprised who or what will come to your rescue once you overcome the awful fearfulness of fear.

"For God hath not given us the spirit of fear; but of power, and of love, and of a sound mind" (II Timothy 1:7).

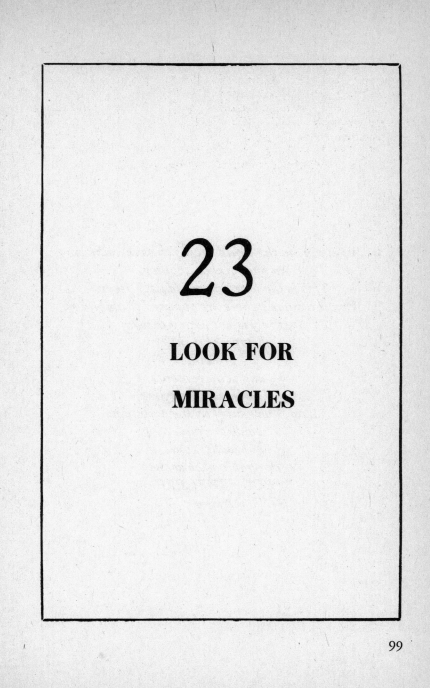

23

LOOK FOR
MIRACLES

Everyone in the world seems to have ambition
in one form or another.
This is the way You made us, Father.
Why is it some people are opposed to ambition?
It surely is not wrong to want
improvement,
growth,
and achievement
...if I don't hurt anyone.
Lord, I will excel by the ambitions
which are mine...
but really Yours.
For behind the scenes
YOU ARE THERE!
Amen.

LOOK FOR MIRACLES

What do you really want in life? What would you say is your number one ambition? What makes you feel good, complete, and whole? If you could have one prayer answered, what would that prayer be? If you could experience a miracle, what would you want it to consist of?

Now all of these questions are relevant and important. You must examine them carefully and honestly. And if you need a miracle, why not ask God for it. Now, a miracle to you may not necessarily seem a miracle to someone else; so, go ahead and ask God for your particular miracle.

But, remember, God must first have something with which to work. Give Him what faith you have, give Him what love you have, give Him what finances you have. Whatever comes to you from God must first have within it a "seed-faith" gift from your life in expectation of His gifts. If it is a miracle of love you need, give a little love. If it is a miracle of money, give a little money. Don't be caught up with the visible; what you can see, feel, and touch. Look away from the obvious, and look to God alone as your source.

Jesus took the five loaves and " . . . looked up . . . " we are told (Matthew 14:19). It was then He fed the people; but only after "looking up." Many of you take your loaves (what you have to work with) and look down in shame. It's no wonder your ambitions are frustrated. You are caught up with lack, need, trouble, heartache, and problems. Look away from all of them to Jesus.

The Bible says, "Looking unto Jesus, the author and finisher of our faith . . . . " (Hebrews 12:2). Learn to see every situation with the eyes of the Holy Spirit. When you are filled with the Spirit you are acting on the fullness of God. God never looks at a

101

situation and says it is hopeless. He would have you look at everything through His eyes of hope and fullness. Again and again He becomes your ambition, your answer to all need and desire.

24

KEEP THE
CHANNEL OPEN

Lord, so many things change through the years,
changes everywhere I look.
But me . . . Lord,
do I change as I grow?
I have a little hope,
a dream which keeps flowing
even though the tides of life,
places and people
change.
You know what it is . . . and will know when it's
finally all fulfilled.
Let all change;
but keep this dream
flowing and growing in me.
Amen.

KEEP THE CHANNEL OPEN

My wife and I enjoy a favorite spot on the shores of Lake Michigan. We started dating there, and over the years we have returned again and again with our family for rest in the beauty of the surroundings.

On a recent visit I took special notice that the shoreline had changed through the years. As I walked along the great shoreline of Lake Michigan, I especially noticed a small, peaceful channel that flowed quietly and steadily in spite of the changing shoreline. The shoreline of the great lake had changed but the channel that fed into the lake at that point remained unchanged.

Time changes lots of things. The waves of the great lake had altered the shoreline through the years. Some things were gone forever; but, the quiet little channel which flows from Silver Lake to the great lake has kept flowing unchanged through the years. It has paid no attention to the changing, restless currents of the big lake with its creeping paralysis on the shore. The little channel remains open, free, and flowing.

I thought as I walked along the little channel that this was like life. Many things on the shores of life change. Some places of joy, others of sorrow, maybe a few of shame are gone through the waves of time; but the little channels of our lives keep flowing.

The hope of the abundant life is that you do not let the changing shorelines affect your channel. Keep the channel of your life open and flowing into the great waters of God. It is the joy of being lost in the whole, lost in the greatness of God, that makes meaning for all of life.

We used to sing the song, "Let Me Lose Myself and Find It Lord in Thee." This speaks of losing yourself in the whole, which is the secret of the enriched and flowing life of being lost but not forgotten.

Is your channel open? Do love, faith, hope and good feeling for God, others and yourself still flow through freely? Or, is your channel clogged by sticks of fear, logs of hate, and debris of unbelief?

Why not take a walk through the channel of your heart and check to see if anything is hindering the free-flowing waters of prosperity, faith the good feelings of joy and the abundant life. Let the shorelines change if they will, but, determine in your heart to keep the channel open. God wants you to flow. He wants life to be filled with the creative waters of living faith.

Remember, if you keep the channel open the changing shorelines do not matter.

25

WHERE ARE
YOUR RESOURCES?

I have that secure feeling
when I know Who my Source is.
There is no undue worry,
fear and
restlessness
when I affirm,
"GOD IS MY SOURCE!"
Lord, how is it You can supply
the needs of so many people
for so many generations?
Today I go off to face the day,
fully aware that all I need
is mine.
You are working!
Amen.

WHERE ARE YOUR RESOURCES?

The other day my son phoned me. He is an avid young man, bursting with enthusiasm and interested in life. In our conversation we began to reminisce about the years he lived in our home and all the different activities in which we had engaged. He said in a happy tone, "You know something, Dad, as a boy growing up I never had the idea—even once—that I was being raised in poverty." He went on in a low tone, "Dad, the Lord has been good to you."

When I hung up the phone I had a sense of satisfaction that my son realized that my resources were not the church or an organization, but my resource was God.

What is your resource today? You need a bigger resource than the banks, loan companies, stock market, or your organization. All of these are good; I thank God for bankers and loan companies who assist us so that we may build better lives, bigger homes and churches.

You need not worry about the energy crisis, the possibility of recession, political cover-ups, the Middle East, or even the Second Coming of Jesus. God has all that on His calendar. You must keep your eyes on your source—God. All your resources are in Him! St. Paul said, "My God shall supply all your needs according to his riches in glory by Christ Jesus" (Philippians 4:19).

All you need to do is to give Him something to work with. Give Him yourself, your love, your faith, your trust. Your resources are in God but you must give Him something to respond to.

When you give God something to work with you are not depending on depression or prosperity in the land. You are not looking to the fluctuation of the cost of living; you are looking to the immovable, unlimited supply from God's hand. You are learning to draw from a totally different resource of supply than the world; it is God's own unlimited ability to meet all your needs. You know this because you are in partnership with Him. Your needs are God's needs. Your work is God's work. You are owned by Him, and it is up to Him to meet all your needs.

He will meet your needs in good times or bad times. He will be your total resource if you will invest in Him today. You must trust His resources as you give to Him. God, in His loving concern, will give back to you, " . . . good measure, pressed down, and shaken together, and running over, shall men give into your bosom . . . . " (Luke 6:38).

Just where are your resources? Once you know where your resource is, there will your heart be also.

26

GET OUT OF
YOUR SHELL

Oh, God, how long have I
remained in my shell,
waiting for someone to free me.
But, You gave me the choice
to be free today.
I will stand up to my world
and declare my freedom.
The incubation days are over
and it's time I went out
to discover the world . . . my world.
It's wonderful!
Amen.

GET OUT OF YOUR SHELL

While our family was enjoying the fast pace of the great city of Chicago, we decided to visit the Museum of Science and Industry. We walked from room to room, excitedly looking at the many varied inventions, creations, spaceships, and living animals.

We noticed a sign which told us that real baby chicks were now being hatched so we headed toward the hatching dispensary. As we stood there looking at the little eggs being cracked open by the baby chicks, we were thrilled to see one that was coming out of its shell. It was a miracle, a marvelous thing to watch life breaking into freedom!

The incubation of the baby chick takes 21 days. This is the time the cell is forming and growing into a live baby chick. Incubation is the quiet state, the unseen development of the chick. And is not to last any longer than 21 days.

Incubation has its limitation. It is the time of life for silently growing to maturity. It is a very important state of birth, but it must come to an end. For, if the chick is not hatched following the incubation period, death is the result. The chick must come out of its shell or the shell becomes its tomb.

The first evidence of the little chick being hatched is a little bulge in the outside shell. The breaking out action is called "pipping." This little bulge in the outer shell is caused by an "egg tooth" on the beak of the baby chick. It is a glorious sight to see the chick coming out of its shell by picking away with the egg tooth.

The egg tooth is used to break the shell. I understand that the only real purpose for the egg tooth is to dig a hole and crack the shell in order to make room for freedom, life, and development. The egg tooth drops off soon after the chick is hatched. If the egg tooth remains ater hatching, the chick will die of starvation. He no longer needs to pick — he is free. The tooth must drop off and make room for the beak to pick up food.

At first the new baby chick looks very unnatural. He appears to be sickly and lifeless, almost dead. But, in a matter of a few hours he is walking around, fluffy, strong and already experiencing new growth. He is out of his shell.

I thought later about the many parallels between the baby chick and the successful life. It is a wonderful thing to watch people start their journey toward freedom. This is the purpose of the new birth, the purpose of God in your life. He wants you to be free! The shells of fear, lack, greed, self, can all be broken. You can have the "egg tooth" of faith whereby you can pick your way out of your shell. Pick your way past the incubation period. Pick your way out of the shell of death and come where freedom is.

There is no need to keep picking at life once you have broken into freedom. It is a great feeling to know you have broken free! It all appears to be unnatural at first as you emerge from your limitations, but in a short time you will be natural and whole. Break the shell and come where freedom is!

27

ONLY BELIEVE

People told me it couldn't be done.
You know something, Lord,
I believed them . . .
for a long time.
But, one day a flash of hope came to me
and I decided to see who was right . . .
my hopes or their despair.
SURPRISE?
I was right . . .
it could be done.
But, what about all the things I didn't do
because of them . . .
Oh well,
bless them anyway
. . . there'll be a tomorrow.
Amen.

ONLY BELIEVE

On one of our visits to Chicago my wife and I decided to visit the world-renowned Board of Trade. So, leaving our hotel on a bright, sunny morning, we walked the six blocks to the Trade Building. There it stood, tall and masterly with people coming and going like bees from a beehive.

As my wife and I walked through the revolving door to the elevator we noticed a sign in the lobby which read, "No visitors allowed today — remodeling taking place in the balcony." The balcony is on the fifth floor and is the only place where visitors are allowed to watch the bargaining of world traders.

We walked through the lobby to the elevators and were told by the elevator boy that it would be utterly impossible for us to get on the fourth floor where the trading was actually going on. He said they would shoot him if he were on that floor!

I said patiently, "Please push the elevator button for the fourth floor."

He replied, "But you don't understand, you can't go there. Only members of the Board of Trade can get in there."

In a friendly tone I said, "Please, push the button for the fourth floor."

"O.K." he sighed, "if you insist."

The elevator came to the fourth floor and Ruth Ann and I got off. She held her breath as we approached the massive hall where the trading was going on. I walked straight to the main desk outside the great hall and told the keeper who I was, where I was from and said, "I would like to see what is going on and observe the action." After hearing my request he asked a big, tall man to sign the approval to get us into the trading center. As he did so the man at the desk said he must get us a coat. (I thought perhaps I was not dressed well enough, but he simply meant everyone on the trading floor had to have a coat of a specific color). Only those with coats of this designated color were allowed on the floor. He said, "Tell the coat-man that Ed sent you." I did and received two coats, one for Ruth Ann and one for me.

In a moment we walked into the air of confusion created by traders from all over the world in the midst of buying and selling.

All the men who were trading in the "pits," as they are called, were yelling as if they were at a football game. Ticker tapes were flying, mammoth billboards with flashing lights were telling the story of the trade gains and losses throughout the world. The cost of wheat, soybeans, and corn from all over the world were being displayed in their movements of gain or loss.

One of the men in the trading pits told me he was just a small buyer. He only bought about three million dollars worth a day! He told of one man who had bought at a crucial time and had gained twenty-three million in one day.

As we left the hall the doorman said we could keep our guest badge as a souvenir.

When stepping off the elevator on the first floor there stood our young elevator operator. I touched his arm and told him my story. He said, "They would shoot me if I did that." I replied by saying, "Son, only believe!"

That is the way with all of life. Believe! Jesus said, "...all things are possible to him that believeth" (Mark 9:23).

How is your believing today? Each day look at the thing you want the most and then say, "I believe! I believe! I believe!" Believe it and it will come to you!

28

CRY AND LAUGH

I had tears . . . still do I cry
when I see a new thrilling sight
or get a sudden "Thud" when
I remember Mom and Dad.
Cry I must . . .
but, laugh I will!
The great balance in living for You,
Lord,
is to be able to laugh and cry
and You know why . . . because
weeping is a part of rejoicing.
While I weep I'll wait
for the tears of rejoicing.
They'll come...
because joy always comes
in the morning.
Amen.

CRY AND LAUGH

There seems to be a connection between crying and laughing. The person who can cry is also the person who can laugh. These two seemingly extreme emotions are tied to one another. It is divine therapy to be able to cry and laugh. Laughter is medicine to the soul; weeping is a washing of the eyes.

My wife wrote a book entitled, *Our First Years*. It is a short history, written in a colorful story form describing our dating, marriage, our first church and many other interesting happenings and heartbreaks in our lives.

A family wrote to us recently expressing their appreciation for the book. The letter said, "This morning, very early, I read your book, *Our First Years*. I cried and laughed as I related your experiences to some of ours. Then I prayed for you, as leaders and parents, and for your children."

The part which struck me in their letter was, "I cried and laughed . . . . " How many times have you heard a story, read a book, watched a television program, or sat in a church service and cried and laughed at the same time? It is an avenue of release and refreshment to the total person to cry and laugh. We are told in Psalm 30:5 "...weeping may endure for a night, but joy cometh in the morning," All of life is not weeping; all life is not laughing. Either of these would destroy the sunshine in the soul and the dew of the night in life. But there is a combination of weeping and joy which keeps life balanced. There is joy in sorrow; success in failure; hope in despair. God sends just enough of each to keep us in touch with the human and the divine. All laughter would make us a poor healer of souls and all weeping would make us unfit to lead others to victorious living.

"Jesus wept" (John 11:35). That is the shortest verse in the

Bible, yet among the most profound. Jesus went to weddings and attended funerals. When necessary He changed the atmosphere of the wedding to greater joy and turned the funeral into a resurrection.

Paul wrote, " . . . we glory in tribulations . . . . " (Romans 5:3). Here is a rare combination, *glory* in *tribulations.*

If God is going to use you, there must be the touch of joy, the touch of hurt, the touch of success, and the touch of failure to your life. The greatest healers are those who know the path of roses has thorns.

Jesus was said to have been, " . . . a man of sorrows, and acquainted with grief...." (Isaiah 53:3). Yet He said, "...Be of good cheer; I have overcome the world" (John 16:33).

It is always amazing to me how the believer can carry a cross and yet have the look of the resurrection on his face, but it's true! If you have the ability to cry you also have the ability to laugh. Don't turn one off for the other — let both flow through your life. You will be richer for doing so.

29

BRIDGES OR WALLS?

Lord, I build walls when I'm afraid.
I've been hurt in the past
and this causes me to hide
behind the walls of self-protection.
I know this attitude is defeating . . .
because when I want to reach out
I can't.
Show me how to take the walls down,
little by little,
and let others into my life.
If I build a bridge for others,
it could be for my own escape
from fear and isolation.
Lord, I'll build . . . no matter what!
Amen.

BRIDGES OR WALLS?

On our 25th wedding anniversary, a number of people sent their best wishes, congratulations and words of encouragement to Ruth Ann and me. One letter said, "You are building bridges and not walls . . . ." That intrigued me— "building bridges and not walls."

I am sure you are familiar with the song, "Bridge Over Troubled Waters." It speaks of my ability to help you build a bridge across troubled waters to a life of safety and security. Bridge-building takes time and demands sacrifice. To build bridges you must forget yourself!

If you build walls, you shut yourself in and people out. Wall-builders are defensive and protective. Bridge-builders are "wayfinders." They are not defensive against life, but aggressive in life.

It is one thing to see people in trouble and quite another thing to build a bridge to help them out of their trouble. When you build bridges for the fainthearted, the troubled, you help them and yourself to reach a destination of security and happiness.

The greatest bridge in the world is the Cross of Jesus Christ. He made a way for us to escape the corruption of the world. We can pass from defeat to victory, despair to help, death to life by the "bridge" of His Cross. It is God's way to happiness, salvation and security.

If you find that you are building walls of separation between yourself and others (walls of defense or fear) why not ask God to help you use the material for bridges instead of walls. It may be a very small thing for you to touch another; but you could build a bridge today that could cause some heartsick person to go from despair to hope.

Not long ago my wife and I stopped to visit a woman nearly 80 years old. She is a widow who lives all alone. We were in a hurry on our way home from vacation, but we took time to stop for a short visit. We found her in the backyard working with her lovely flowers. She graciously showed us her flowers and talked of each of them with tenderness. We went to the strawberry patch, picked a few berries, ate them together and rejoiced in their goodness. She cut flowers for us to take home and loaded us down with homemade bread and cookies.

Inside the house we sat at her little table and held hands for a short prayer. After prayer we hugged each other and said good-bye.

A few days later a letter came from her. In her own handwriting she said, "You will never know the burden you lifted from my heart the day you stopped to see me. I can't express my deep appreciation for your visit and prayer."

Just a little time and love built a bridge to help this lady over her troubled waters that day. That's what building bridges is all about.

What kind of building program are you in—bridges or walls?

30

ARE YOU LUCKY?

There was a time
I felt lucky . . .
then I lost.
It looked like a loss . . .
at the time.
The losses overshadowed the wins . . .
so I concluded I was a loser.
I would have remained in this
frame of mind;
But You, Lord, healed my heart!
Now I know I'm favored . . .
really lucky.
All is well . . . I cannot lose.
No one can who is
trusting and trying!
Amen.

ARE YOU LUCKY?

Now wait a second before you say you don't believe in luck.

I'm sure some of you have an inner response that wants to reject the word, "luck." But before you turn me off, let me explain.

If you don't like the word "lucky" then try the words: fortunate, blessed, chosen of God, favored by the Lord. It is not the word I want to stress, but the concept, or principle, *behind* it.

Do you feel favored in life? Do you feel chosen of God?

I was talking to a highly successful businessman not long ago. He said, "When interviewing a man for a job I always ask the question, 'Do you feel lucky?'" He went on to say, "If a man feels lucky (or favored) he has a positive mental attitude about himself, his life, and personal affairs. But if he feels unlucky he will, no doubt, make a poor salesman and project a poor image of his own personal worth and achievement."

I thought on that concept for many days and finally concluded he was right. Show me a person who feels he's a failure, rejected and unlucky and you will discover nothing seems to go right for him. On the other hand, show me a man who feels chosen, blessed and favored of God and he carries an attitude about himself that causes others to say he is lucky. He has a sense of favor, prosperity and good will.

The Bible is loaded with stories of persons who received "favored blessings." God ordained favor for His people. As you read the story of Abraham you will be impressed with the hand of favor that blessed him in all he did. He seemed to be "lucky" in all he undertook, even though at times he seemingly chose the less appealing opportunity when making a decision between himself and others.

This same principle is found in the life of Moses. Even though Moses suffered and was rejected he was still chosen to be raised in the palace of the Pharaohs. Later, he was chosen to be called out of the wilderness as the great leader of the Exodus.

Examine the lives of Joseph, David, Job and hundreds of others who had God's blessing on their lives. Favor — a "streak of luck" — seemed to be theirs.

Why? Does God show favoritism? Is He partial in His gifts? Should we think that God chooses some people and rejects others? No, because our "luck" is all up to us! Not the place where we were born, the color of our skin or the arrangements of the stars, but our own undertakings and attitudes make us triumphant or defeated.

Some questions we might ask ourselves are:

Do I truly believe?

Do I really try?

Do I really see by faith what I am asking for in my prayers?

Nothing of fortune, luck or blessing will come to us when we only pretend to trust or to commit.

The thoughts or attitudes you project will determine the prosperity and blessing that will come to you.

Do you carry within you the feeling of rejection, or do you face people, situations and places with the "favored blessing" of God on your heart?

Do you feel life has been hard? Is there an unspoken attitude of hopelessness, failure and defeat within you? If so, then one of the first things God has to settle in your mind is that you are chosen, blessed, and favored. You will have good success in all you undertake to do. Remember that!

The "lucky" ones seem to be the people who *expect* a miracle.

I think there are several evidences which can be seen in the life of the people who feel lucky or favored:

(1) THERE IS THE ABILITY TO ALWAYS COME BACK AFTER A LOSS OR BLOW. They know the difference between giving up when they ought *to* and not giving up when they ought *not* to. It is senseless to refuse to give up on some things and even more senseless to give up on others. I believe the person with "luck" knows the difference.

(2) THEY HAVE A BALANCED UNDERSTANDING OF

THEMSELVES AND THEIR IMPORTANCE. There is a balance of humility and self-acceptance. All rejection or all acceptance can be dangerous to growth and favor if not properly balanced. The people of "luck" seem to know how to balance humility and self-acceptance.

(3) THEY ACCEPT OTHERS WHO ARE FAVORED. They are not afraid to applaud other successful people. They share their success and are happy to share the success of others.

31

HOW DO YOU
ATTRACT
STRANGERS?

I feel all people are estranged to me,
when I don't show love.
But when I love strongly,
the friendship becomes strong!
Why do I let the old feelings
of suspicion come over me
when I see a face I don't know.
Maybe they feel the same toward me.
Or, do I create
this feeling of alienation.
"I was a stranger and ye took me in."
I'll do the same, too, Lord.
In your Name!
Amen.

HOW DO YOU ATTRACT STRANGERS?

We landed in a lovely private airport at 2:00 a.m. and quickly settled in for a beautiful two-day vacation at St. Charles, Illinois.

We spent the next day swimming and relaxing in the sun, and then enjoyed a glorious dinner by candlelight, rested and happy.

As we left the dining room we noticed a grand piano in the lobby. Ruth Ann sat down and began to play softly. The motel was full of distinguished-looking people, hurrying back and forth through the lobby and down the hall. No one was around the old piano as the sounds started floating gently down the halls, through the corridors and into the outer lobby.

A most gracious lady, wearing a long linen gown, stopped and said, "How wonderful." It wasn't long before a man stopped, and soon an elderly couple started down the corridor toward us with smiles and a trace of tears. The music kept rolling out and the people kept rolling in. After a while a number had gathered around the old piano and were singing happily and enthusiastically (many times off key) the familiar tunes Ruth Ann played.

While the people sang I talked with a very striking, elderly couple and found he was chairman of a group of twenty people who had come from Alabama on vacation.

It wasn't long before someone from the group asked Ruth Ann to play "Amazing Grace." We had already sung everything from "The Farmer in the Dell" to "Old MacDonald Had a Farm" and here we were singing "Amazing Grace" and then "The Battle Hymn of the Republic." I thought to myself that someone here knew something of old-time religion.

135

As the people sang I spoke again to the elderly man and asked about his faith. Sure enough, he was "born again." He had that winning look in his face.

He said, "I've been a deacon on my Board for many years. I built the new church and parsonage for my Pastor and people."

I turned to the striking-looking gentleman and asked, "What is the greatest thing God has done for you?"

Without hesitation he answered, "God gave me three great children who are saved."

"How did this come to pass?" I asked.

He replied, "I took them to church, I took them fishing and I loved them. And, if they needed it and I had it, I gave them a dime when they asked for it."

I showed him the pictures of my children and shared the great joy they were to me, too. In a moment of time we had met and loved each other as strangers, yet brothers in Christ.

The next night Ruth Ann left the motel room for the main desk to secure some stationery. In a few minutes she came back, bursting with laughter and said, "Do you know what? That whole bunch is down there in the lobby waiting to sing. They have been there an hour just waiting for me to come and play for them." And back she went!

I planned to read and rest a while, but suddenly I was reminded of this Scripture, "...I was a stranger, and ye took me in" (Matthew 25:35). With that I got dressed and headed for the lobby. When I arrived, sure enough, there was my wife surrounded by a crowd of people, singing and rejoicing, having a good time.

After witnessing and sharing love with those people we walked back to our motel room. I thought again of Jesus' words, "...I was a stranger, and ye took me in."

What does it mean to be a success? It means going where the need is and being willing to invite strangers into our lives!

32

NO REGRETS

O, Lord, how fast is life!
The years are gone!
Where did they go?
The first house,
the first days,
the kids . . . their cats and dogs;
all the fun (and sorrows)
all are gone.
I stand in the ashes of yesterday . . .
today.
What can I do about regrets?
There shouldn't have been any . . .
but who's perfect?
So . . . I'll let the regrets go.
Where? Into the ocean of love!
There they are . . . hidden from all eyes . . .
even God!
Praise You!
Amen.

NO REGRETS

St. Paul said, "I have fought a good fight, I have finished my course, I have kept the faith" (II Timothy 4:7).

Jesus said while on the cross, "...It is finished...." (John 19:30).

As John Wesley lay on his bed dying he shouted, "The best of all is, God is with us!"

All of these men were saying, "I have no regrets!"

Another climactic day had come for our family. A turn in the road had to be made. My son was to be married tonight. All the preparations had been made. Gowns, clothes, bow ties, candles, rice, cake, punch, coffee, all the trimmings were ready. Pictures were taken, kisses were freely passed out and encouraging words were given.

Many asked, "How are you, Pastor?"

"Fine, wonderful," I would reply.

It seemed my wife and I were doing great. The wedding was over, and at midnight we left the church for home, the place where our son had grown through the testing high school years. It was good to get home and pull off our shoes and relax. We finally pulled the covers up at 1:30 a.m. and fell asleep — Mom and Dad — happy, but tired.

The next morning I went downstairs to clean up for the day. Nobody was up; I was by myself. I had thought I was ready to face this new experience. But suddenly it hit me — my son was gone. His room was empty, his clothes were not in the closet, his shoes were not in the middle of the floor, his pants were not laid over the couch. His bed — that too was gone. I thought, no longer will I hear my son come through the front door at night and call, "Anybody home?" No longer will he come to my bedroom, open the door and say, "Chet, can we talk?" (My father's name was Chet and Steve adopted that nickname for me.)

I thought to myself, as I walked from room to room, "He's really gone, my son is gone." Then, with tears filling my eyes, I stood in his room and said, "God — God, I'm glad I have no regrets. I did all I was able to do for him. I gave him all I had. I did my best. Now he's Yours. No regrets, I have no regrets."

This is God's hope for all of us. He longs for us to have no regrets. Regrets erode away at your life unless they are forgiven.

When I left my pioneer church in San Antonio, Texas, and headed for Waterloo, Iowa, with my family I said to one of the men, "I did my best."

Let it be the goal of your life to give your best. Seek to be honest and truthful with God, yourself, your family and your employer. Someday you're going to leave it all, so make it a rule of your life to have no regrets. You may have failed, you may have made big mistakes; but let the intent of your heart be true and pure. Let your motives be good. Then you will be able to say to yourself and to your world, " . . . I have kept the faith."

The Life that Wins is a life without regrets!

33

THE HEALING
OF MEMORIES

Lord, how can You forget so much?
My file drawers are full of memories . . .
some are sweet,
others are sour.
There are times when the images of the past
show up in the present,
which brings me inner pain.
I can't forget!
. . . or won't!
I wonder if all these painful memories
can be healed . . .
Only by the hand of God!
Touch my inner mind!
They are turned to beauty!
I can live with them now, Lord,
because You have taken the
sting out!
Blessed Jesus!
Amen.

THE HEALING OF MEMORIES

Many of your memories are negative and painful. So I believe one of the most important areas of life is the healing of memories.

What you think is what you do and, most likely, what you'll eventually become. No doubt you are today, both in character and achievement, what you have been thinking on for many years. Your memories become your motivation, either for good or bad.

There are many people who believe they cannot survive the pain of their memories. They feel there are hurts and losses which cannot be forgotten. They're caught in the habit of going around in circles thinking on their past.

Memories can be monsters! But memories can be sweet, too, a treasure for the future!

If you will be honest with yourself, you know that harboring negative thoughts causes most of your suffering and much of your defeat. You have the idea these bruises and hurts cannot be healed. You speak of them more than any other matter when you are alone with a friend. You refer to them in moments of depression and despondency. These memories are with you at all times. You can't forgive. You can't forget.

There must be a healing of your memories or life will not have any success or satisfaction. This healing must go deeply into your mind and spirit where the depression, or hurt, began. If you can recall where the hurt, depression or anger started, there is a good chance you can be cleansed and freed from it all.

I remember when I was a college student. I was what they termed, "Student Pastor." The opportunities for preaching were always before me from the very moment God called me to preach.

I took my first pastorate as a new husband while still in college. The little church was about 15 miles from the campus and grew rapidly under my leadership. There was a constant spirit of renewal for the three years we were there.

This created opportunities for preaching all over the state. Ruth Ann and I would sing and preach as much as we could handle physically while I kept up with college studies and she taught school. We were busy, happy and blessed.

We were new in the Conference and in the church world. Not long after I joined the Conference I was elected President of the state youth group, a large and demanding place of leadership.

I soon sensed feelings of jealousy, resentment and rejection building up toward me in the minds of three or four of the younger pastors. There were many times when I chaired the Youth Board in an atmosphere of deep resentment and jealousy. It was very difficult.

For the first time in my young life I realized not all the church world believed in promotion, growth and leadership! It was as if I had awakened to a whole new world surrounded by religious concepts with a painful awareness that not everybody had love in their hearts. I was rudely awakened to the stark reality that others could, and would, actually hinder and seek to cause me to fail, if it were possible. All this left a pain that was deeper than I thought. I reasoned at the time that none of this was really getting through to me — but it had. My heart was young, tender and full of the Spirit's ambition, and all this conflict left a deep scar.

After some time I moved out of the Conference and took a pioneer work in another state. The problem was left behind — or so I thought. But those feelings of jealousy, rejection and resentment had made a deeper impression on my heart than I realized. And, had I not had these memories healed by retracing them in my mind with Christ, I would have carried them all through my life. I went all the way back to the very beginning and walked through each event in my mind, one by one, with Jesus. I am now healed and free from the past and its problems, the pain and disillusionment.

An emotional healing sets you free to achieve and create. You become free and dynamic after the healing of memories. It's a glorious experience.

Whatever hold your background has on you which causes defeat, sorrow and heartache, trace through it with Jesus. Let Him start right where the agony started. Then walk slowly and carefully through it with Him talking with Him, step by step through all the years to the present moment.

Let Him heal you from every disappointment, heartache, pain, loss, sin and guilt!

34

YOU CAN CHANGE
UNDESIRABLE
CONDITIONS

I wonder if undesirable conditions are sent
to make me grow?
I don't think I would pray
or work as hard
if all my conditions were perfect.
Lord, You have mysterious ways to
improve my conditions . . .
the people I work with,
the house I live in
the conditions I just can't stand
are meant to be.
So, thanks! It's the unfavorable
which has caused me to change.
I'm glad, Lord, You put me in
the place I was . . . so I can be in
the place I am!
This is Your wisdom!
Amen!

YOU CAN CHANGE UNDESIRABLE CONDITIONS

There are times in life when you seem to be the victim of some undesirable condition. You feel your condition is stagnant and unmoving; everything is at a stalemate. But, you can change this undesirable condition into a golden opportunity by changing your attitude.

St. Paul was in an undesirable, dark and damp prison. He could have felt self-pity, rejection and loneliness, but instead he started to sing. Singing opened the doors of his soul as well as the door of his cell. I'm sure Paul wanted to continue to travel, preach and be on the go. But most of his later years he sat alone in a Roman jail writing simple letters. What a poor way to influence the lives of people! Nothing to do but write letters.
How could this ever influence the world? Such a poor way to communicate! But, he changed the world!

Everything must have the balance of cause and effect in your life. Everything which happens to you comes as a result of something else. It may be undesirable, but look for these undesirable conditions to produce tremendous opportunities. The cause of every situation is found within the situation. Once you find the cause you can change the effect it has on you.

Situations are only as undesirable as you permit them to be. There is always a way through every undesirable condition. The laws of God, the laws of love, harmony and good are supreme! They must work for your good.

Most adverse and painful conditions are a result of disobedience to these laws. To reverse undesirable conditions, see if you have misused God's laws in your life. Determine what caused your undesirable condition in the first place.

If you have broken any laws or principles, repent quickly and turn to the higher law of love and obedience. These undesirable conditions are to teach you, train you and make you superior to all situations. Learn to work with the laws of love, honor, respect, and these laws will work for you as well.

You are not chained by circumstances. You long for greater opportunities, answers to prayer or a more useful life. All this longing is good. All can be yours if you will change your attitude toward undesirable conditions.

See your circumstances as a schoolmaster driving you closer to Christ and the Bible. Your conditions force you upward and onward. Let them make you strong instead of sour.

Someone said, "You may bring about the improved outward condition which you desire if you will unswervingly resolve to improve your inner life."

Persevere down the road of good, forgiving attitudes and useful hands, and golden opportunities will come to you. Great friends, who may be strangers at this moment will show up in your life to help you. Sympathetic hearts will be drawn to you. Books, ideas and finances will begin to respond to your heart because you are living above undesirable conditions. This is the power which will eventually change the conditions.

Someone once said, "Perhaps you are living in a small cottage and are surrounded by bad conditions and you desire a larger and nicer place. Then you must ready yourself by making your little cottage a paradise as much as possible. Cook your plain food with all the care possible and arrange your humble table as tastefully as you possibly can. If you cannot afford carpet, let your rooms be carpeted with smiles and love, fastened down with the nails of kind words."

Ennoble your present surroundings by ennobling your heart. You will rise above them as you do. Ennoble what you have now and you will be more greatly enabled in the future. Do not look to anyone or anything at the moment; but look to God. He will bring you up, out and over your undesirable conditions.

35

FEELINGS
MAKE THE
DIFFERENCE

Feelings are fun . . . sometimes.
There are times when they hurt me
and others.
It seems feelings really color
my thinking,
my praying,
my hoping.
My feelings are like the waves
of the ocean . . . always changing.
I suppose that's the reason God gave
me feelings . . . so I could enjoy
(or endure)
the changing moods of living.
Lord, I'll not fight my feelings,
I'll only try to understand them...
if I can!
But, if I don't understand, I'll wait...
for tomorrow they will
change into another color.
Amen.

FEELINGS MAKE THE DIFFERENCE

How you feel about something or someone makes a difference in what you do.

Emotional responses can cause you to either favorably react or to completely reject a person or situation. Your feelings are as colors in a rainbow, a frame around a picture or a touch of perfume on the ear—the extra touch that makes the difference.

There are many destructive emotions which can make life dull. Let's take a look at some which, if given an opportunity, could take hold of you mind.

Some are: irritation, anger, hurt, worry, sorrow, hate, fear, bitterness, suspicion, resentment, depression, prejudice, greed, lust, unforgiveness, jealousy. These destructive emotions remind me of a bed of rattlesnakes — one of them could strike at any moment if you are not cautious. Any of these emotions can weigh you down, cut the fiber of your faith, and shut off the flow of abundant life.

Your life reflects how you feel! It is impossible to hide your feelings, you must recognize and regulate them. Feelings play a large part in the motivation of living.

We respond to all of life, at times, by *moping, doping, groping* or *hoping*. These responses either help us *cope* or *cop-out* on life. There are millions of people who would rather cop-out with a tranquilizer, a drink or a big spending spree than to cope with life. Running away from your feelings is just as bad as letting your feelings run away with you. Feelings are important!

But, there are constructive emotions as well which you must learn to deal with in life. Here are a few: love, forgiveness, release, encouragement, hope, faith, praise, acceptance, forgetting past wrongs. If you will replace the destructive emotions with their opposites, you will soon know the winning life.

Try this: in place of fear — put faith. In place of confusion — composure. For hate — love; unforgiveness — forgiveness; inferiority — self-confidence.

Someone said, "We get rid of a destructive emotional attitude by consciously developing the opposite constructive feeling."

In other words, whatever feeling you don't like, you develop the opposite attitude in its place. Do the very opposite of your destructive emotions and you will feel the difference right away. Use every means possible to develop good, constructive feelings and attitudes in you life, for the river of feelings runs deep.

Remember this verse, "...A river of water of life...flowing out of the throne of God...." (Revelation 22:1). Here is where all good, healthy feelings originate. Hold to the image of His mighty river of life flowing through you for your good.

Feelings can make the difference!

36

THE POWER
OF PURPOSE

You know, Father,
when I have a worthy purpose
I feel important.
When my purpose meets the needs
of others
there comes with it
a sense of destiny.
What is Your purpose, God?
It's big, I'm sure!
What is my purpose? Why
am I here?
When I find my purpose I seem to
have found Yours.
I wonder if all purposes of heaven
and earth
don't tie into each other . . .
if they're good.
I know this,
a purpose that is worthy
brings success.
Let all succeed . . . Amen!

THE POWER OF PURPOSE

The great difference between people, the feeble and the strong, the great and the small, is a powerful purpose. It's the invincible determination of purpose to do or die that gets results. It's win all or lose all.

The most important element is not what you *were* or what you *want to be* but what you *are*. What you are building today is the basis of your success tomorrow. If you succeed an inch each day, it won't be long until you've completed the first mile.

The progress of purpose creates the joy of succeeding!

Where do you want to be five years from today? What plans have you laid? What about your home? What about your children? Just where are you going? There is a productive power in a meaningful purpose.

There are four reasons why most people fail in life. Let me urge you to avoid them.

(1) CONCLUDE YOU ARE DOING ABOUT AS WELL AS THE NEXT PERSON.

If he's your standard of performance and he isn't doing much it's likely you won't do much either. Sometimes you say, "I'm doing alright." But, compared to whom are you doing alright? That makes a big difference in the effort to succeed.

(2) YOU USE THE AVERAGE AS THE STANDARD OF PERFORMANCE.

The average person works 40 hours a week, takes the weekend off, and seldom does more than is expected. That's the pattern of complacent failure. It's a dead-end road, and many are just simple enough to follow that kind of pattern. Abraham Lincoln said, "Expect the impossible of yourself and everybody who works with you." I believe that!

(3) YOU TAKE YOURSELF FOR GRANTED.

You don't know how much ability, talent, and courage there may be in you. You have never been put to the full test of your abilities; therefore, you don't know what they are. You have not been challenged to try and try again. You've been programmed to just "get by" and that's all. But the person who has a purpose finds power, talent and insight he never knew were hidden in his inner heart. The energy is there and you'll find it pouring forth as you do more than is required.

(4) YOU HAVE NOT DECIDED WHAT YOU WANT.

This is one of the great pitfalls in life. The Bible says, "...a doubtful mind will be as unsettled as a wave of the sea that is driven and tossed by the wind; and every decision you then make will be uncertain, as you turn first this way and then that." James goes on to say, "If you don't ask with faith, don't expect the Lord to give you any solid answer" (James 1:6-8 The Living Bible).

Solid answers, solid progress, solid success is found in a solid purpose!

You need to make up your mind there isn't any good reason why you can't succeed in life. God is for you! Life is for you! Many of your friends are pulling for you! You need to pull for yourself as well!

When you find a need and seek to fill it, you're on the road to success. The greater you seek to meet other people's needs, the greater will be your satisfaction and sense of fulfillment. Lend your efforts to finding needs, troubles, inconveniences, then seek ways to solve them.

This is the reason we pay the doctor almost anything he asks. He has met our need. The reason we pay a big price for food, rest, automobiles, or any other pleasure, is because our needs are being met.

This is also the reason many of you give to churches and missionaries—you have enlarged your heart and your need is being met. Somebody is meeting your needs. These are the people we support. Empty restaurants, cold churches, failing and divorced homes all point to the fact that someone is not meeting the need.

Once you have a purpose, commit yourself to it. Let nothing

stand in your way. Commitment is a sure way of bringing a purpose to full birth and maturity.

The Bible instructs us, "Commit thy way unto the Lord; trust also in Him; and He shall bring it to pass" (Psalm 37:5). Man purposes, but God brings it to pass!

Make your plans!

Make them big!

Make them in the light of the world — it's a big place, you know.

Once you have made your plans in prayer, faith and confidence, trust God to bring it to pass. He loves success! God is the God of life, creation, and expansion.

All through the Bible God has instructed you to " . . . lift up your eyes . . . look on the fields . . . enlarge the place of your tent . . . lengthen your cord . . . strengthen your stakes." He is saying in effect, "Grow — develop — do — go — become — multiply!"

The man who created the first shopping center in the world said, "Make no little plans. There is nothing in little plans to stir men's blood. Make big plans. Once a big idea is recorded in your mind it can never die!"

Jesus said, "...you have been faithful over few things, I will make you ruler over many...." (Matthew 25:21). The power of purpose succeeds!